Using Natu

by Ma... Lee

PEARSON
Scott Foresman

DK

What are natural resources?

How Resources Are Used

We use natural resources to make what we need. We also use natural resources for energy.

Natural resources are the materials we get from nature. Some natural resources are living things, such as plants and animals. Some resources such as soil, water, minerals, and sunlight, were never alive. Air is an important natural resource. All natural resources help support life on Earth.

Living things need natural resources. Plants must have air, sunlight, soil, and water to grow. Plants and animals give people the resources they need for food. Everything we eat, use, or buy either is a natural resource or is made from one or more natural resources.

Renewable Natural Resources

Earth has renewable and nonrenewable natural resources. Renewable resources can't run out. They can be replaced. **Solar energy** is power that comes from the Sun. It is renewable. Air, water, trees, and soil are also renewable natural resources.

Water is a renewable natural resource.

Why Soil Is a Renewable Resource

Soil covers most of Earth's land areas. Some animals and plants make their homes in the soil. Animals and plants provide food for other living things, including people. Soil is a nonliving natural resource.

How Soil Is Renewed

Rock breaks apart during weathering. Plant roots and ice erode rock by breaking it into pieces. Wind and water carry bits of rock and deposit them in new areas. After a long time, broken rock becomes soil.

Plant roots cause rock to crack.

More plants growing weathers the rock even more.

Ingredients in Soil

Soil is made of bits of weathered rock. Soil contains humus. **Humus** is decaying plant and animal material. Humus adds nutrients to soil.

Some animals, such as prairie dogs, dig entire towns under the ground. Tiny organisms such as bacteria, fungi, worms, spiders, and insects, also live in soil. They break down plant and animal remains that plants can use as food.

Different soils come from different kinds of rocks and minerals. The amount of humus in soil affects its color and how it feels when you touch it. Soil samples from different parts of an area can look and feel very different.

Larger plants grow in the soil that has formed.

Topsoil is the top layer of soil.

Subsoil is part soil and part rock.

Bedrock is mostly solid rock.

Properties of Soil

Each kind of soil has certain properties. Topsoil has a lot of humus and bits of weathered rock. These bits can be different sizes.

Clay, Silt, and Sand

Clay is soil made mostly from the smallest bits of broken rock. The materials in clay make it different colors. Red clay has bits of iron in it.

Silt is soil with slightly larger particles in it. Silt feels smooth. Sand is soil with even larger particles. Sandy soil has bits of different materials. Quartz is the most common material in sand.

The color of sand depends on what materials are in it. Some sand is tan. Sand from volcanic rock can be black.

Clay

Silt

Sand

Soil for Growing Plants

Plants grow best in soil with many nutrients. Sandy soil does not hold nutrients. Clay can hold nutrients. But it is so hard that most plant roots cannot spread very easily. The best soil for plants has some clay, silt, sand, and humus.

Soil as a Renewable Natural Resource

Some plants can put nutrients back in soil. Plants that get plowed under at the end of a growing season also renew soil. Renewing just a few centimeters of nutrient-rich topsoil can take 1,000 years. That same amount of topsoil can wear away in only ten years.

Other Uses of Soil

Soil has many uses besides farming. Clay is used to make tile, bricks, and pottery. Sand is used to make concrete, glass, and other things.

How are resources used for energy?

Renewable Energy Sources

People use energy in many ways. We use energy to run machines, make heat, and grow food. We can use the Sun's energy without even trying. A room becomes warmer when sunlight shines in.

Solar energy warms Earth. The air near Earth's surface heats up when it meets the warm ground. The cycle of heating and cooling air makes wind energy. The Sun also powers the water cycle by making water evaporate.

Solar panels take in energy from the Sun. Solar cells in the panels turn the energy into electricity.

How We Use Solar Energy

A **solar cell** changes energy from the Sun into electrical energy. Solar cells are put together to make large solar panels. Fields of solar panels collect energy. Solar energy is changed into electric energy or heat energy.

In a solar heat system, solar energy heats water. The heated water runs through solar panels into a storage tank. A pump forces the water into pipes. The hot water can be used to heat buildings.

Energy from Flowing Water

Moving water has energy. Today people use this energy to run machines that make electricity. Dams are built to control how the water moves. Water forms a lake behind a dam. It flows through gates in the dam when its energy is needed.

Nonrenewable Energy Sources

Some resources are nonrenewable because they are used up faster than they are put back naturally. Others cannot be replaced at all. People use many nonrenewable resources for energy. Ore is a nonrenewable resource. **Ore** is a rock that is rich with minerals.

Fossil Fuels

Coal, natural gas, and oil are nonrenewable energy sources. They are fuels that we burn for heat. **Fossil fuels** come from organisms that lived long ago. The Sun is the source of energy stored in coal, oil, and natural gas.

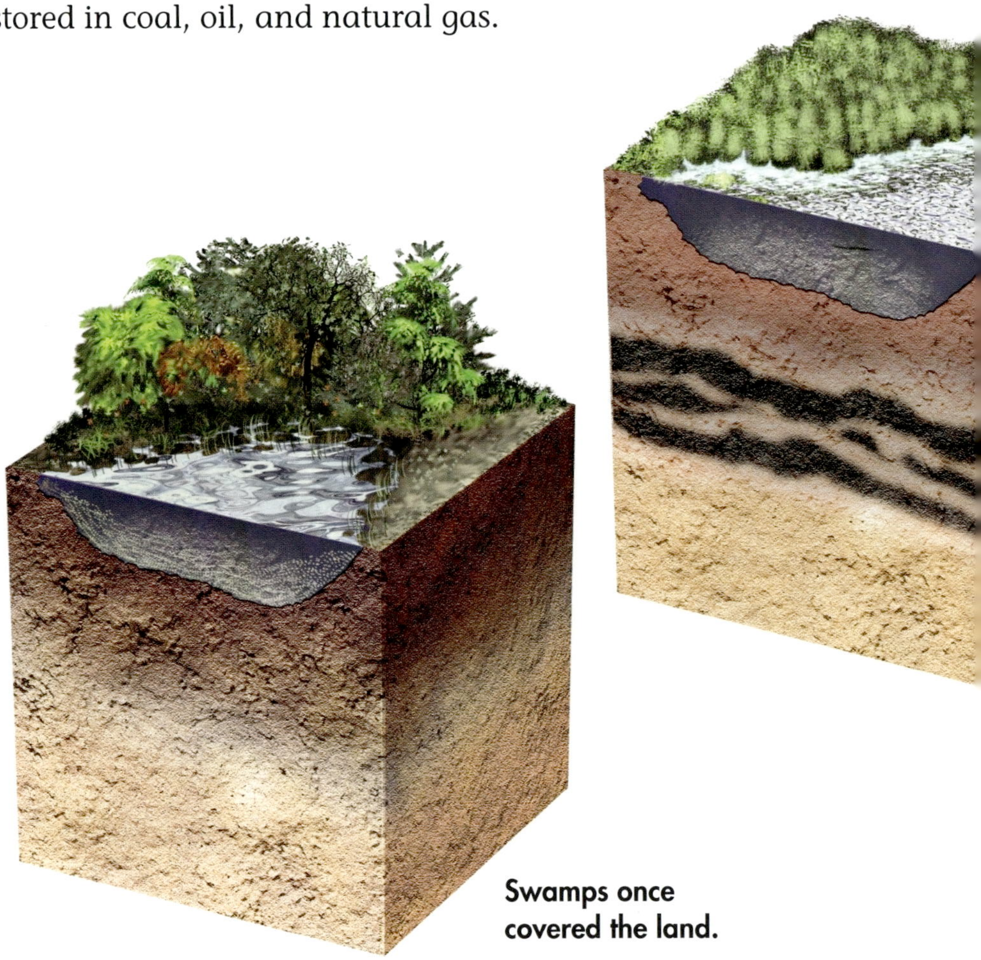

Swamps once covered the land.

Petroleum is commonly known as oil. Petroleum is made from ancient sea life. Bacteria, algae, and other organisms used the energy in sunlight to live. Their bodies stored energy they didn't use. After they died, their remains fell to the ocean floor.

More and more dead organisms fell to the ocean floor. They formed thick layers called sediments. Millions of years passed. The heavy top layers pushed down on the lower layers. Pressure, heat, and decay changed the remains. Chemicals in the bodies of those tiny organisms turned into fossil fuels.

Impact of Fossil Fuels

Removing fossil fuels from under the ocean floor can harm Earth. An oil spill can result from drilling under the ocean. Oil spills kill sea life. Spills can also kill or harm living things along the coast. Companies are working to make drilling safer and cleaner.

Using fossil fuels also has harmful effects. Air is polluted when fossil fuels burn. Too much carbon dioxide in the air may lead to global warming. Gases from burned fossil fuels can break up in rainwater to form a weak acid. The acid falls to Earth as acid rain. It can damage buildings. It can harm living things.

This oil rig digs deep into the ocean floor to get petroleum.

How Resources Can Last Longer

People use nonrenewable resources to meet most of their energy needs. But as people need more energy, fossil fuels will be used up faster than ever. Fuel costs will go up.

Water, air, soil, and trees are resources that help all living things. We must use them carefully. We must not waste or destroy them. It is hard to restore forests, soil, and fishing areas. It costs a lot of money too. So does cleaning up polluted air, water, and soil.

To help our fossil fuels last, we can use less energy. We should also use wind power, water power, solar energy, and other renewable energy sources.

Old tires can be used to make a wall.

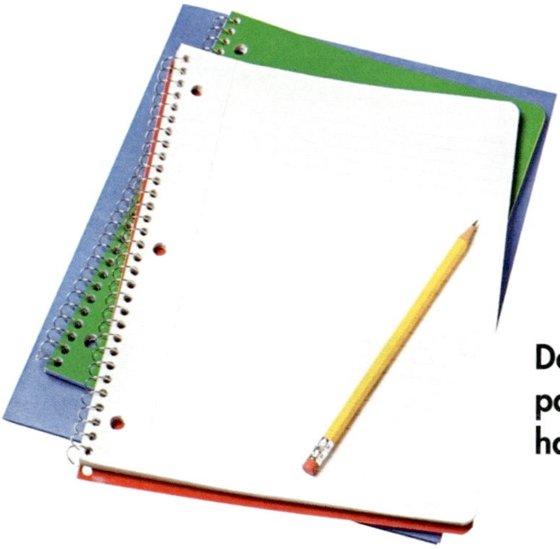

Do you recycle paper? The paper in a notepad may once have been your newspaper.

Methods of Energy Conservation

Conservation means using only what you need. When you conserve, you use resources carefully and without wasting them. You can cut back energy use in many ways. You can walk or ride a bike to go short distances. For longer trips, you can share rides with others. Turn off lights you don't need.

Some cars and appliances use less energy to do the same amount of work as others. Less energy is needed to heat buildings that have good insulation. If we conserve energy, our resources will last longer.

Nearly everything in this car's trunk can be recycled.

Recycling

Recycling is saving, collecting, or using materials again. Recycling helps us reuse raw materials. There are ways to recycle glass, cardboard, aluminum, tin, paper, steel, and some plastics. Look for the recycling symbol on containers before you throw them away. It looks like three arrows chasing each other around a triangle.

Nature provides many materials that support life. These natural resources help us live and grow. Some can be renewed. Others will be used up someday. It helps all life on Earth when people use natural resources wisely.

The recycling symbol shows materials that can be reused.

Glossary

conservation	the act of using only the resources you need without wasting them
fossil fuels	nonrenewable resources that come from the remains of organisms that lived long ago
humus	bits of rich soil formed from the decaying remains of living things
ore	a rock that is rich with minerals
petroleum	another name for the fossil fuel commonly known as oil
recycling	saving, collecting, or using materials again
solar cell	a device that changes energy from the Sun into electricity
solar energy	energy that comes from the Sun